About Face

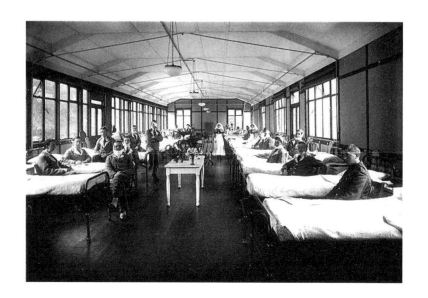

About Face

World War I Facial Injury and Reconstruction

Ann Gerike

FLOATING
BRIDGE
PRESS

Seattle, Washington

My thanks to the editors of the following journal and anthology, in which the following poems first appeared: *Floating Bridge Review:* "My Husband, Now and Then"; *Alehouse:* "Transformation" and "Speechless."

Cover design: Anita K. Boyle, Egress Studios

Floating Bridge Press
909 NE 43rd Street, #205
Seattle, Washington 98105
www.floatingbridgepress.org

Frontispiece: British Ward, the Queen's Hospital, 1917–18.

All the photographs of the facial surgeries performed on Robert Davidson, Sidney Beldam, and Walter Fairweather on pp. 29, 30, and 32 are reproduced courtesy of The Hunterian Museum at the Royal College of Surgeons. The cover, frontispiece (p. ii), and the photographs on pp. xv–xvi of the introduction, as well as the two later Davidson photographs on p. 28, are reproduced courtesy of Dr. Andrew Bamji. The three photographs of Sidney Beldam in later life on p. 31 are reproduced courtesy of Marilyn McInnes.

Readers interested in learning more are directed to the Gillies Archives website, *www.gilliesarchives.org.uk.*

For the men whose surgical records
inspired these poems,
and for all who have suffered facial injury
while serving their countries

Contents

Wedding Portrait, 1926

For Lillie Helene Grobengieser Gerike (1904-1983) and Marcus Gustav Gerike (1900-1975)

When my father met my mother, he fell in love
despite her sunken jawless cheek, or because of it;
because after years of pain she still could laugh;
because he was in love with all things medical
and all things new, and plastic surgery was both;
because the surgeon who'd excised the festering bone,
his skills sharpened by the war, would soon replace it
with her floating rib, she her own Adam.

A year and six months later, both my parents face the camera.
My father stands in formal suit, bow tie, head tilted
in his wife's direction. A flower-filled cloche meets
her dark eyes, a swirl of veil pools at her feet,
her white satin short-sleeved dress falls waistless,
tucked up below her knees. She smiles the smile
of any virgin bride, her pleasant unremarkable face
turned slightly toward what she would call her good side
for fifty-seven vigorous years.

Acknowledgments

Throughout this project, Dr. Andrew Bamji, FRCP, Gillies Archivist to the British Association of Plastic, Reconstructive and Aesthetic Surgeons, generously shared his unmatched range of information and knowledge about facial injury and reconstruction in World War I, first at the Gillies Archives in 2008 and more recently in his verification of this book's accuracy. To him my undying gratitude. In addition, he is a genial man, a prolific composer of very funny medical verse, and, like Harold Gillies, a practical joker.

My heartfelt thanks to the poet-teachers of Whidbey Island, Washington, especially Lorraine Healy, the Argentine-American poet (*The Habit of Buenos Aires*), under whose expert, humane, funny, culturally broad, and generously affordable guidance I and the other members of her ongoing seminar developed and honed our unique poetic sensibilities and skills, and to my fellow poets in her group.

Thanks also to Alan Hawk, historical collections manager at the National Museum of Health and Medicine in Silver Spring, Maryland, for sharing a treasure trove of historical information about American facial surgeries in both the Civil War and World War I; and to Wayne Larrabee, MD, a poet and humanitarian as well as editor of the *Archives of Facial Plastic Surgery* (American Medical Association), in which my commentary, "World War I and My Mother's Jaw," was published in October 2012. Gratitude as well to Rod Suddaby of the Imperial War Museum, London, and Stephen Logsdon, librarian at the Washington University School of Medicine in St. Louis.

A residency at the Hedgebrook Writer's Center in 2008 enabled me to sink my teeth into the project, and a GAP grant from Artist Trust of Washington enabled my travel to the Gillies Archives that year; my gratitude for both. Pat Barker's remarkable *Regeneration* trilogy opened a door into the world I was just entering, and innumerable friends and acquaintances, even strangers, provided leads to new material and new insights, as well as practical computer help. The fine editors at Floating Bridge Press, especially Kathleen Flenniken, maintained and expanded their interest in a manuscript that was twice a finalist in their annual chapbook competition. A special thanks to John Pierce for his patient and meticulous editing and his book design.

Women appear infrequently here, but without their courageous work as nurses, members of the Volunteer Aid Detachment (VADs), and ambulance drivers in primitive battlefield conditions, the successful treatment of these men could not have been accomplished. Ironically, their work is more widely recognized, through their own writings and books about them, than that of the facial surgeons, whose creativity, inventiveness, artistry, and genuine caring have largely been lost in the shadows of their surgical skill. And in this book of white faces, also unacknowledged are the many people of color—from overseas dominions, dependencies, and possessions of Britain and France, as well as from the United States—who fought for, worked with, and provided essential services for the Allies.

My thanks as well to Riel Holbrook and Helen Ludwigson. Shirley and Maurice Samuelson, my lifelong friends in London, have frequently fed, housed, nurtured, entertained, and when necessary clothed me, and Maurice, with his journalistic background, has been an invaluable English connection in this project. My broadly knowledgeable son David Robinson has been a touchstone throughout, as a reader, computer guru, and gentle commonsense advisor. Thanks to all of my surviving family—David, Peggy, and Cathy Robinson; their husbands and partners Jay Pascucci, Shirley Braunlich, and Sam Nicholson; my grandchildren Jeremiah and Maggie Nicholson; and my sisters Esther Brockmann and Eunice Eckerly—for being who they are.

Introduction

The literal loss of face is a subject fraught with poetic implications, and threat. When the recognizable storefront is gone, how will others be able to know what's inside? And even worse, unless you avoid mirrors and all reflecting surfaces, including the faces of others, how will you know yourself? Whatever else we may claim—about our souls, our spirits—at some deep level most of us see our bodies, and especially our faces, as our essential selves.

Wars have always produced their share of facial injuries, but the First World War can claim the lion's share. It was the first large-scale war fought with mechanized weaponry, and it followed closely enough on the heels of a different kind of warfare that the generals used antiquated battle tactics for too long, ordering huge numbers of men armed only with rifles and bayonets to charge across open fields into the enemy's gunfire. Even John J. Pershing, the Commanding General of the American Expeditionary Forces in Europe, initially pursued similar tactics with his troops in 1918 despite hard-learned advice from the British and French.

It is impossible to give an accurate count of that war's facial injuries. The estimate of 280,000 is overwhelmed by the total estimate of dead and wounded military—9,720,000 dead and 21,228,000 wounded. Most histories of the war scarcely mention facial damage as a separate form of war wound, and none that I know of at this time fully acknowledge the remarkable reconstructive surgeries on which many of these poems are based.[1]

The majority of facial casualties were inflicted on the Western Front, those roughly parallel lines of Allied and German trenches that eventually made their tortuous way 450 miles, from the North Sea in Belgium and Flanders all the way down through France to the Swiss border. In the first month of the war, September 1914, the Germans, unable to advance and already skilled in trench warfare, dug in first, on higher ground near the River Aisne in northern France, and the Allies dug in across from them.

And so a trench system developed along the line of battle, the German trenches deeper, better equipped, and better protected than those of the Allies. A no-man's-land of as little as fifty yards or as much as half a mile separated the rolls of barbed wire protecting each line. After months and years of shelling, many of the Allied frontline trenches (originally between seven and eight feet deep, five to six feet wide, and shored up with timbers and protected with sandbags) were little more than ditches, often filled with mud or water and occupied by dead bodies, or pieces of them.

A trench line was really a rabbit warren of trenches—a zigzagging front line connected with secondary and tertiary lines for bringing up supplies and soldiers, and carrying back the disabled and walking wounded to field hospitals. The front was not always active, and men were rotated through these trenches when fresh troops were available.

For three and a half years it was stalemate, with the Allies on the offensive. Each side gained and lost no more than a few miles in a series of battles fought on flat boggy ground, on rolling wooded hills, in chalkland, in dense sucking mud, in freezing cold and searing heat, in downpours and blizzards as well as on serene blue-sky days. Heavy bombardments preceding battles could last a few days or even a week or more, lighting up the sky at night. The noise was deafening.

Men in the trenches might be shot by snipers, but the majority of facial injuries were incurred on the battlefields. Many facial wounds were caused by the new high-powered rifles and machines guns, but those caused by artillery—mounted projectile-firing guns that had never before been used so intensively—were the most devastating. Shrapnel, the most common form of artillery missile, consisted of a hollow shell packed with small steel or lead balls and gunpowder and managed by a timed fuse—in effect, a very powerful shotgun with a very wide range. A 75 mm shrapnel projectile contained 270 steel or lead balls, the 155 mm version, 800 of them. Shell fragments, also referred to as shrapnel, tore flesh and bone apart. Essentially the same weapons, including chemical gases, were used by both sides in the conflict.

Although the rebuilding of faces, especially noses, has a long history dating back to 800 BC in India, its primary use in Europe before the war was to repair defects caused by genetics, disease, or injury.[2] At the outbreak of World War I, the European continent boasted several renowned facial specialists, including Hippolyte Morestin in France and August Lindemann in Germany, but Great Britain had none. By the end of the war, however, the British were leaders in facial reconstruction. This change was due primarily to the work of one man, Harold Delf Gillies (1882–1960), who became a major advocate of the need for this specialized service, and also a skilled, innovative, and caring facial surgeon.

Born and raised in New Zealand and trained in England, at Cambridge, he was a member of the Royal College of Surgeons and an ear, nose, and throat specialist when war was declared. In 1915, at the age of thirty-two, he joined the Red Cross (then a branch of the British army) and was sent to Wimereux, in France, to monitor the pioneering facial surgeries of a wealthy and flamboyant French-American dentist, Charles Valadier, who had established an army unit there for the treatment of jaw injuries, the first of its wartime kind.

The work captured Gillies' imagination. It posed surgical challenges, the need to restore the complex and interrelated functions of the nose and mouth so that men whose facial features had been blown off would be able to breathe, eat, and drink. It also appealed to him for aesthetic reasons. In his writing, he referred to his work as a "strange new art." Known for

An operating theater at the hospital, Major Harold Gillies is seated on the right.

his physical dexterity as a sportsman—he had been a champion cricket player, a first-rate rower, and remained an avid golfer all his life—he also was a competent amateur painter who in later life had a London exhibition.

While in France he obtained permission to observe Morestin performing surgery on a patient with advanced facial cancer, using the latest skin-flap techniques for facial reconstruction. And at about this time he met an American dental surgeon, Bob Roberts, who lent him a German book on the topic of jaw and mouth surgery that further stimulated his interest.

When Gillies returned to England, he persuaded the army's attorney general to establish a "Plastic Unit" at the Cambridge Military Hospital in Aldershot, Hampshire, on the southern coast. To ensure that men with facial injuries would be sent to the unit, he designed his own casualty tags, had them printed at his own expense, and sent them to the War Office for delivery to the field hospitals. The patients arrived.

But after July 1, 1916, the first day of the Battle of the Somme, which left two thousand men with facial damage, he convinced the head of army surgery of the need for a much larger establishment. With the purchase of Frognal House in Kent, south of London, and its large estate, that dream was realized, and in 1917 the Queen's Hospital for the facially wounded was dedicated.[3]

The house itself, which still survives, dates from the early eighteenth century. It became the chief hospital and the residence of the operating physicians and nurses, while sturdy prefabricated buildings were erected on the spacious grounds for bright and airy window-lined wards, convalescent hospitals, rehabilitation training, residences for other staff and

workers, and eventually shops and a post office—all the essentials of a small village. The wounded men worked on the farm or were trained in more than forty different occupations, often with their faces bandaged. Toy making was the most popular and received the most attention from the press. Those who

Aerial view of the Queen's Hospital, 1917 (Frognal House is not visible).

had been blinded were trained to be masseurs, boot repairers, and poultry farmers, among other occupations; their faces were repaired with as much care as those of sighted men. Together the patients played sports, had picnics and parties with nurses and female employees, were shown films regularly, and were entertained by actors, musicians, minstrel men, and comedians. They also entertained themselves.[4]

The medical staff was organized on national lines, with the British, Canadian, Australian, and New Zealand units established separately, each keeping its own records. Gillies was a pioneer in the team

Rooftops of the wards.

approach: the surgeons, both medical and dental, as well as anesthetists, nurses, and even portrait artists (who were helpful in planning surgeries) met regularly to discuss cases.[5] Dentists were particularly important in the treatment of jaw injuries, which occurred with great frequency.

Once the war was over, the number of patients declined, and the larger enterprise was closed down by 1921. But the transfer of patients from other hospitals, and the need to continue whole series of operations—in effect, repairs of previously unsuccessful repairs—resulted in Gillies and his team providing plastic surgery to injured soldiers there until 1925. In the eight years of its operation, the hospital admitted and treated more than five thousand British and Commonwealth servicemen.

The files of their surgeries—photographs and case notes—were long assumed to have been lost, as the Ministry of Pensions destroyed all medical records in the late 1920s, when pension calculations had been finalized. That we have them now is largely because of the interest and efforts of Dr. Andrew Bamji, a rheumatologist who was appointed to the modern Queen Mary's Hospital at Sidcup in 1983, at a time when the hospital's past was just beginning to emerge. Aided by serendipitous events and chance meetings, he became the recognized expert on the subject of the surgeries, writing and speaking about them frequently. In 1989, records of the surgeries performed in the New Zealand unit of the Queen's were shipped to him from that country. He spoke on the subject at a medical illustrators' gathering in 1992, and shortly thereafter Gillies' records resurfaced in the photographic department of Queen Mary's Hospital in Roehampton, where he presumably had placed them. Bamji was, of course, notified, and it was he who brought order to the files (not all of them complete by any means) and negotiated the formation of the Gillies Archives in the Postgraduate Education Centre on the hospital grounds.

In addition to the photographs and case notes, Bamji amassed a comprehensive library of books on medicine and surgery of the Great War, including many relevant to facial surgeries, some of them rare or hard to find. Gillies, in his two-volume work *The Principles and Art of Plastic Surgery* (1958), written with Ralph Millard, discusses many of the operations in greater detail, adding personal touches about the patients and their families. I had the good fortune to visit the center in 2008 and spent several days there, learning from Bamji's encyclopedic knowledge of the subject as well as studying the original files.[6]

From the photographs, it is abundantly clear that not all operations were successful, especially in the early days, when surgeons were dealing with fresh wounds, hastily treated at field hospitals, sometimes infected. The situation at the front was chaotic, with huge numbers of wounded men pouring into the hospitals. Out of necessity, triage was developed, with the mortally wounded separated from those with a better chance of survival. Unless head and neck injuries were also involved, facial wounds alone were not usually life-threatening. The men often arrived at the Queen's a week or more after an injury.

Surgeons had to be creative; such wounds in such numbers had never been dealt with before. They had to learn on the job. In his book, Gillies often describes what he learned from his mistakes, including operating too soon because the patient was impatient. He also describes his invention, during a surgery, of the pedicle tube, a method of skin grafting that greatly improved outcomes and is still in use to some extent today.[7]

Both the early problems and the later advances are demonstrated in the notes and photographs of Private Walter Fairweather, the son of a platelayer for the Great Northern Railway, and are the subject of one of the poems in this collection. On his first hospitalization, between July 15, 1916, and October 4, 1917, he had seven operations attempting to repair his nose, mouth, and the eyelid of his missing eye, all of them ultimately unsuccessful (and only one of them by Gillies). An undated photograph from this period shows Fairweather with a bulbous half-nose swung to one side, a swollen upper lip and perpetually open mouth, and three dark eyelashes apparently growing under the depression where his left eye had been. It seems he refused further surgeries, for he was discharged in January 1918 ("Total result: Unsatisfactory") but advised to return for further treatment.

In February 1920 he did return, and after nine more operations between February 23, 1920, and July 7, 1921, several of them using the pedicle tube, he was discharged with a rather large nose (which would shrink with time as the swelling went down), a normal-looking eye socket, and a closed, ordinary-looking mouth.

Learning to look directly at photographs of the initial injuries without revulsion, especially those of the initial injuries, took me some time. But as I read the case notes, especially when the surgery was extensive and well documented, I began to see the men as full human beings with damaged faces rather than as facial monsters. And I began to imagine stories for them, to get under their skins.

I could never have done that solely from my own experience. I am an almost-eighty-year-old American woman at the beginning of the twenty-first century; they were young British men at the beginning of the twentieth. I come from a family of Lutheran ministers and have never known anyone well who fought in a war. I simply was not interested in wars, though in 1965 I had been greatly moved by the sardonic music-hall version of World War I presented in Joan Littlewood's *Oh, What a Lovely War,* which my English husband and I saw at the Theatre Royal, Stratford, in the East End of London.

Like most Americans, I knew less about World War I than World War II. So I began to read widely and soon realized that I could, to some extent, immerse myself in the experience of the battlefront soldiers through the wealth of written materials left behind. Their letters and journals, now residing in museum and library collections, as well as their memoirs and those of others involved in the war, have been extensively mined by historians, documentarians, and writers of every stripe. Their memories have been explored in interviews collected in books and shown on television. Together, these convey a fuller experience of the war than any study of politics or battles, strategies, and statistics could possibly provide—not only the horror and terror of battle, of "going over the top," of living with death, dismemberment, and destruction, but also the sheer physical exhaustion, the acute discomfort of life in the trenches (mud, cold, rats, lice), and the long stretches of sheer boredom. Battles did not go on nonstop, and soldiers often found themselves in quiet zones, where they simply stopped trying to kill each other, with the agreement of their officers. The well-documented and often-dramatized "Christmas truce" of 1914 was unusual in that it included the prolonged intermingling of troops in no-man's-land.

What made the war more bearable (in addition to alcohol and cigarettes) was the camaraderie. In that war, as in any, ground troops fought for each other, not for abstract principles. And in World War I, many men were in battalions with old friends, having been encouraged to join up as "pals." These were young men, after all, and a mordant and irreverent sense of humor had helped many, especially the large numbers who had lived in poverty or semipoverty, to survive at home. This war was the first to be thoroughly photographed, in both still and motion pictures, by amateurs and professionals alike, and it is surprising how often the men are smiling in informal photographs taken on the battleground when the fighting was not active.[8] No doubt the smiles decreased over the years as the killing continued and the men became exhausted.

While a great many survived to live out what seemed a normal life, they were all changed, and large numbers remained hospitalized with shell shock.[9] How many committed suicide is uncertain; their deaths were often attributed to other causes, to spare the family.

Some of the writers of that period are well known—Robert Graves, Siegfried Sassoon, Wilfred Owen—but the trenches were full of men who wrote letters to family and friends and kept journals even after they were forbidden to do so. They were a remarkably literate and well-read group. Universal state education in England and Wales was introduced at the primary level in 1870 and the secondary level in 1900, with a thorough grounding in English literary classics. This was also a time when the appeal of popular education and "self-improvement" was at its peak.[10]

My interest in the facial surgeries, and the war, developed late in life. But it had its origins in my childhood, and my mother's left jaw. Born in 1933, I grew up with the story of her miraculous 1925 surgery in a St. Louis hospital, when she was twenty-one and had just met my father. Her diseased jawbone was neatly replaced with one of her floating ribs by a "world-famous surgeon" in St. Louis.[11] He had tucked the scar under her jawline, and she was not defaced in any way.

Because she was a born optimist, she presented it as adventure rather than trial, despite the fact that, according to her dentist, she had been experiencing considerable pain and swelling for a year or more before the surgery. She would even move the unhinged jaw back and forth with a hand to entertain me and my brother and three sisters (I was in the middle of five) and our friends. Though not a vain woman, she would always turn her head toward her "good side" for photographs, and I have only a few casual shots of her from the left. A woman of great energy and spirit, she lived to seventy-nine—with all her remaining teeth. Her surgeon had told her that her rib-jaw would not bear the weight of a dental plate, so her dental care was scrupulous.

Although I and others in my family have an abiding interest in medical matters, and though the records of her hospitalization, including bills and two letters from her surgeon, eventually turned up, none of us had been curious about the surgery itself. Had we been able to examine it from a fresh and disinterested point of view, we would no doubt have realized that it was far more advanced for its time than seemed possible.

My mother's surgery became less of a miracle, and much more interesting, when in 2007 I learned about the English artist Paddy Hartley's Project Façade.[12] It was on his website that I first saw the case notes and photographs of the faces damaged in World War I. Suddenly, something my mother had once told me—her surgeon's remark that hers was the first jaw he had removed before replacing it—made sense, especially when I learned that he was chief of the Oral and Plastic Surgery Department of the US Army Corps during the war and a renowned maxillofacial surgeon even before then. His name rolled off the tongue: Vilray Papin Blair.

In his book, Gillies records "a group of three American observers, including Vilray Blair of St. Louis, Missouri" visiting the Queen's Hospital late in the war; he adds that they returned home to establish units of their own.[13] I have a newspaper article from a 1919 *St. Louis Star-Times* with a photograph of the two men, each expressing admiration for the other, taken during a hospital-visiting tour Gillies made in the United States that year. Both are described as leaders in the new field of facial plastic surgery, already beginning to be used for beautification as well as repair.

Interestingly, the tin and copper facial masks created during World War I to cover irreparable damage have received more widespread attention than the surgeries. A few of them were created at the Queen's Hospital. The work of skilled portrait artists, they were remarkably life-like, molded to the wounded man's face, and were almost always attached with spectacles, having been made to cover partial damage rather than the entire face. Hot in the summer and, of course, unchanging over time, they were not a success, and none have survived. They have great dramatic potential for fiction and theater, perhaps because a horror imagined creates a frisson of fear more tolerable than a direct gaze at the horror itself.

World War II, with essentially the same weapons but a different style of warfare, produced some facial injuries but many less than its predecessor. Gillies was called back into service in 1941 and did his work at Rooksdown House, the private annex of a hospital near a small town called Basingstoke, in south central England. Because of his efforts, the house eventually became a haven for veterans and others with irreparable facial damage, some of them his former patients. It was at Rooksdown that Gillies performed the first female-to-male transgender surgery, in seventeen operations between 1946 and 1955.[14]

A much younger cousin of Gillies, Archibald McIndoe, whom he had trained, supported, and encouraged, became well known in Britain for his work on the faces of burned airmen in World War II. He insisted that his patients become part of the local community and formed the Guinea Pig Club, whose reunions were regularly documented in British newspapers through the years.

In the subsequent twentieth-century wars, facial injuries received little if any publicity, although the rate of maxillofacial wounds in the Korean War was almost as high as that in World War I.[15] The facial damage in the ten-year period of the recent Iraq and Afghanistan wars, though infrequently mentioned, has been more widely acknowledged than any since World War I, with several front-page articles in the *New York Times* and occasional media coverage. Between eight hundred and nine hundred US combatants have suffered serious facial damage, primarily from improvised explosive devices (IEDs). Those whose faces were severely burned required not only facial reconstruction but facial restoration, and thus far only a semblance of normality has been achievable for most.[16]

The majority of us can see a person without an arm or a leg, or arms or legs, and if the person's face is intact, we still see a human being. But when we see someone whose face does not look human, our instinct is to look away in shock and horror, and possibly disgust. It is hard for us to face up to what has happened to them in these wars waged in our name.

The ironies remain enormous—the search for more effective, efficient, and deadly means of inflicting bodily damage and death, accompanied by the search for more effective and efficient means of healing injuries.[17] Do we really need the first to accomplish the second?

Notes

1. Jay Winter and Blaine Baggett discuss the topic of facial injury, along with other war injuries, at some length in *The Great War and the Shaping of the 20th Century* (New York: Penguin, 1996), 364–71. However, they apparently were unfamiliar with Gillies' work and the Queen's Hospital surgeries.

2. In the United States in the 1860s, a military surgeon, Gurdon Buck, performed several documented reconstructive surgeries on the faces of soldiers injured in the Civil War. As the first industrial war and the first to utilize modern weaponry on a large scale, the Civil War produced many injuries similar to those of World War I. Buck was the first military surgeon to document his results using pre- and post-operative photographs. He also used plaster casts, several of which are on display at the National Museum of Health and Medicine in Silver Spring, Maryland, along with casts and displays documenting facial surgeries in World War II and the Vietnam War.

3. The many hospitals established and named for Queen Mary at this time were all designated "The Queen's Hospital" and identified by their location, in this case Sidcup; it was informally called "the Queen's." "Mary" was added to the name later to distinguish these hospitals, or new ones established on their grounds, from those established under subsequent monarchs.

4. The nature of facial wounds (a term that excludes those of the head and neck), as opposed to bodily ones, likely made for a more active life at the Queen's than at other military hospitals.

Because of the excellent blood supply to the head, facial wounds bleed profusely and are less prone to infections than many bodily wounds; they also heal more quickly and, because of the absence of large muscle tissue with its network of nerves, they usually cause less pain unless the severing of bone is involved. There are several accounts of soldiers being unaware of facial wounds until they encounter another person. Many of the facial surgeries, especially the later repairs, involved only soft tissue and were performed with local anesthetics. While wound-related difficulties with eating and breathing could be life-threatening and cause great discomfort, a relative absence of postoperative pain, coupled with the lack of bodily injury, allowed a much greater variety of patient involvement on the hospital grounds.

No doubt the camaraderie of wartime also existed at the Queen's, where the men lived in close quarters in an essentially closed community and shared the same affliction. (The nearby village of Sidcup had little to do with them; in fact, park benches designated for hospital patients and their visitors or attendants were painted blue to warn village residents of what they might encounter there). A farcical playbill by the Thespian Society survives, complete with tongue-in-cheek advertisements, announcing "*The Patient's Dream or A Visit to the Theatre,* in 1 Act and Several Groans," set in "A Facial Hospital in Nightmareland."

The blindness, both temporary and permanent, caused by mustard gas, one of the several poison gasses used on the Front, is much better known than that accompanying facial injury. I know of no statistics separating the two. It has been noted that the blind were the happiest group in the hospital, not being confronted constantly with the visual evidence of loss, but their lives outside of it must have been more difficult.

5. Not only was Gillies a world-famous surgeon, he was also a personable man, cheerful and generally well liked despite his predilection for practical jokes (which may have accounted for his not being knighted by the British government for his services until 1930). A free-and-easy colonial rather than a member of the British upper classes, he seems to have been a natural egalitarian, and his concern for a private's face was as great as that for a soldier of higher rank. His development of the team approach seems a natural outcome of his character.

6. Unfortunately, the center was closed and its contents dispersed in 2012 as an austerity measure. The photographs and case notes of the surgeries are now in the possession of the Royal College of Surgeons in London, and the library is housed in the Brotherton Library, University of Leeds.

7. Previous to the invention of the pedicle tube, most grafting at this time involved either taking a flap of skin from a distant site on the body or lifting skin from a nearby site and folding it over. Because the lifted skin lacked a blood supply, such grafts often failed. During the 1917 operation, Gillies realized that, when he lifted the skin and allowed it to roll itself into a tube, as it did naturally, he could keep it alive until it was needed by leaving it attached at its source, stitching it shut along the long edge, and reattaching it near the site where it would be used, allowing it to grow there for a time. He then detached it from its source and somersaulted it into place, opening the tube and using the still vital skin. Early on, such grafts were sometimes made using skin from more distant parts of the body and transporting it up by leap-frog stages, a tediously long and uncomfortable process for the patient.

Gillies does not seem to have been greatly concerned about public recognition, but he was unhappy when he found that the invention of the pedicle tube in 1917 had been claimed by Vladimir Filatov, a Russian ophthalmologist, who first published the finding. Apparently the idea was more or less simultaneous for the two men. Gillies describes it in his book as occurring on October 3, 1917, when he was operating on "an Able Seaman by the name of Vicarage" with severe burn injuries. He would be pleased to hear that, in non-ophthalmological circles, it is sometimes referred to as the "Gillies Flap."

8. Max Arthur's *The Faces of World War I: The Great War in Words and Pictures* (Cassell Illustrated, 2007), an impressively extensive collection, illustrates this point admirably with images of men from a broad array of the armies involved, in a wide variety of situations, occasional smiles intermixed with the more frequently reproduced images of that war's unimaginable carnage. Pictures of one's own dead, dismembered, or horribly disfigured, or those of one's allies were never shown—a long tradition until recently, when

frequent users of the Internet encounter or are able to access photos of bodily and facial injuries considered inappropriate for general viewing by an older generation.

9. Michele Barrett, *Casualty Figures: How Five Men Survived the First World War* (Verso, 2007), is the best brief account of the war's conditions and its effects on those who fought in it, particularly interesting because it is based on the men's personal histories, both pre- and postwar. She notes that when trench warfare ended in the spring offensives of 1918, rates for shell shock fell sharply. The Oxford scholar Niall Ferguson, in *The Pity of War* (Basic Books, 1998), a detailed, passionate, and controversial study of World War I, discusses shell shock in his vivid description of the conditions the men survived (340-42). He notes that after the war, approximately 65,000 British ex-soldiers were drawing disability pensions because of "neurasthenia," as it was then called, and 9,000 were still hospitalized.

10. This information is from Paul Fussell's *The Great War and Modern Memory* (Oxford University Press, 1975), which brings together a wide variety of historical and literary material pertinent to the war.

11. The floating ribs are the two lowest ribs, attached neither to the sternum nor to the cartilage of other ribs. The exact source of my mother's problem is not clear. In the family, it was often said to be osteomyelitis, a bone inflammation, but was sometimes blamed on two "buried" wisdom teeth. A November 1923 letter to my mother in Altamont, Illinois, from her local physician, Dr. C. M. Wright, refers to "the apparent enlargement in your left lower jaw [which] has subsided in a large way . . . not continuing to expand and get larger and weaker as it was doing when you first came under our observation. The multiple cystic process appears to be stationary. . . . This bone cyst damage is behind the area of the buried teeth in this jaw and extends clear up to the joint in front of the ear."

My mother's surgeries were about a year and a half later. Dr. Blair, in a postsurgical letter to Dr. Wright regarding swelling in the area, for which my mother was briefly hospitalized, says: "I do not believe it is part of the original tumor; it doesn't behave like it, and that tumor should not come back." Whatever the cause, it must have been a difficult and painful time for her, but she never talked about her suffering.

12. A constant theme of Paddy Hartley's inquiry in his career is how the human face and body are or can be transformed by injury or intent, and the ways we respond to that transformation. His focus in Project Façade was on the facially wounded individuals, and he even followed up with some of the descendants of the patients. His 2008 exhibition "Faces of Battle" at the National Army Museum in London included both textile works and a wall of the facial photographs. My discovery of his project was timely, as I had fallen in love with the craft of poetry not many years before I was told of his website in my poetry seminar, shortly after I had talked about my mother's jaw surgery.

With the centenary of the war approaching in Europe, interest in the injuries and repairs is increasing rapidly in England, where it was a minor plot-device in an episode of television's *Downton Abbey.* Hartley has expanded his project, and two recent novels, both highly acclaimed, are set in part at the Queen's Hospital: Louisa Young's *My Dear, I Wanted to Tell You* (HarperCollins, 2011), and Pat Barker's *Toby's Room* (Doubleday, 2012).

13. Unfortunately, there is no treasure trove of individual photographs and case notes for the American maxillofacial surgeries comparable to the material in the Gillies Archives. However, they are documented in a 161-page article compiled by the surgeon general's office, published as a chapter in volume XI, *The Medical Department of the United States Army in the World War,* 1923–29. It includes the contributions of nineteen medical, dental, and surgical specialists. A statistical count of wounds notes 2,970 to the cheek, 2,184 to the eye, 1,123 to the lower jaw, and 670 to the nose, and chapter discussions are organized around those areas of surgery. A fascinating and thorough medical and surgical compendium, it is liberally illustrated with before-and-after photographs and includes several references to Gillies' work.

It also includes this description of the Free Rib Graft, which my mother apparently received:

> In using this method a piece of rib, generally the seventh, was resected in the usual way . . . care being taken not to open the pleural cavity. This was trimmed to proper length and inserted between and in contact with the previously prepared mandibular fragments, being fastened to them with silver wire or kangaroo tendon. A green stick fracture could be made in the piece of rib to simulate an angle or curvature of the jaw.

A stated advantage of this method is that "the rib is porous and easily penetrated by new vascular supply. It could be readily made to conform to the natural contours of the jaw, and large gaps could be spanned."

14. See Pagan Kennedy, *The First Man-Made Man: The Story of Two Sex Changes, One Love Affair, and a Twentieth-Century Medical Revolution* (Bloomsbury, 2007). Her description of Gillies is basically unflattering and sometimes misinformed; he definitely was a practical joker and became more eccentric with age, but he was also a compassionate man and did not have the slapdash, carefree attitude toward his surgeries that her book implies.

15. Rates of facial injury in the Korean War (often called "The Forgotten War," though fourteen nations took part) were 14 percent, almost as high as those in the First World War; see Robert Love, Tom H. Brooking, and Darryl Tong, "The Management of Maxillofacial Trauma during the Korean War—A Coming of Age of a Specialty," *Journal of Military and Veterans Health* (August 2011): 10–14. Rates were lower in Vietnam. To my knowledge, there was little if any publicity about these injuries during either war.

16. The *New York Times* articles appeared on August 22, 2007, and January 21, 2012. In Caroline Alexander's "The Faces of War" (*Smithsonian,* February 2007, p. 78), Dr. Joseph Rosen, who notes that a former colleague had trained under Gillies in World War II, states that IEDs are to this war what artillery fire was to World War I, but because of their much greater concussive force, the facial injuries are much more severe. When a vehicle explodes after encountering an IED, the facial burns are devastating. Repairs now include partial face transplants and great improvement in facial prostheses with artificial skin technology. Robotics experts are also becoming involved.

17. We have become so accustomed to antibiotics that a frequent reaction to first hearing of a successful early twentieth-century facial surgery is astonishment that it was accomplished without them. World War I was, however, the first war in which more combatants died of gunfire than of disease. In many ways, both medicine and surgery were more advanced at the time than most of us give them credit for, especially in their use of antiseptics and anesthesia. Of necessity, wartime surgeons developed new methods in both the early and later treatment of projectile wounds. The development of Dakin's solution, a long-sought wound antiseptic, saved many lives. For anesthesia in surgeries, older anesthetics such as ether, nitrous oxide, and chloroform were used, as well as local and intratracheal anesthetics. By the end of the war in 1918, administration of intravenous fluids (blood, plasma, salines) was common.

About Face

Harvest on the Somme

July 1 to November 19, 1916

They were mown down efficiently,
those green recruits, those working men
of Britain, laden with 65-pound packs,
120,000 ordered to step trimly
from the trenches into the front lines,
rifles at the ready, bayonets set,
to advance into the cutting blade
of machine-gun fire at walking pace
in even lines, strictly spaced at intervals
of 100 yards, to step sharply
over the windrows.

That first day, 20,000 British dead,
40,000 missing or wounded, 2,000
faces shattered. But Haig still held
stockpiled supplies, broad fields
of healthy men, all the necessary
machinery.

Month after month the mower ground along,
inched forward 7 miles. A harvest echoed
from the other side.

No granary could store 600,000
men, no gleaners could recover
all the scattered flesh,

so from that flesh, those bones,
golden wheat has sprung,
is springing.

Photographs from the Queen's Hospital

I look askance at this sea of mangled faces,
eyes awash in flesh, cock-nosed, slam-mouthed,
slice-tongued, hearing in the trenches
the roar of war, the whizbang's
whistle. There flies a nose, an eye
gone south, all disbanded,
released from active duty, free
to shoot over whatever sea of muck
might suck them in.

These men look at me straight.
No bog-fallen ones here.

Keep your eyes on the eyes, I say,
for that's where the man resides,
where you'll catch sight of him
despite his flimflam face.

Return the favor.

Transformation

He was an ordinary bloke, a talker
with a storage-shed brain, glad to fling
the doors open, hand you helpful hints
on lice picking, trench-popular parodies
of hymns—"When This Lousy War Is Over,"
"Forward Joe Soap's Army"—until
the gunshot got him, sheared away
his chin, and his mouth's floor.

Now, at the Queen's Hospital,
bare-chested, head torqued right and up,
his pose recalls a Christ
crucified.

His dark eyes devour the distance.

The shed is flooded, bloodied, rats scrabble
on the floor. No parables possible,
no way to bless and eat
the broken bread.

Growing Faces

It's Bosch-like, this garden,
men planted in hospital beds
in uniform rows. Tube pedicles,
living cylinders of a man's own skin,
crawl down from foreheads,
up from chins and necks
like pale headless caterpillars,
leaving trails of scars.
Attached at last to trellises of bone,
they may become a nose,
a jaw, a chin.

Patiently the surgeons graft
to return exotics to the unremarkable,
the unremarked.

Private Fairweather, Age 22
Wounded July 1, 1916

Dimpled chin, right eye and forehead
perfect. Across the left eye, stitches march,
turn sharp left down the scarred face, pass
the absent nose, and halt at the right upper lip,
tracing the bullet's path. The open eye is empty.
No viewing of last week's battle available.

Gradually a face materializes—an eyelid,
followed by a lashless eye. The private's spirits rise;
in one photo, still cockeyed, his good eye is laughing,
his carp-like mouth has its parenthesis of curves.
Soon it segues to closed lips, kissable; the artist
sketching nose plans draws him grinning.

Then an elongated darkness, a cave-painted animal
in flight, leaps across his shaved forehead, marking the place
from which the skin was lifted for a pedicle. Above his right ear,
a stalk sprouts, drapes under his eye, across his cheek,
roots itself on the nose's bridge. Finally the stalk is gone,
has flowered into an almost perfect though still-swollen nose.
After five years, sixteen surgeries, the now-civilian private
has a face.

He marries, settles down, has children, grandchildren.
He is a wonderment to them. Small curious fingers
trace his facial scars, admire his manufactured nose,
gently prod his shrunken eye. He makes a story of it,
tells them the funny bits, nothing nightmare-producing.

His face settles slowly, like an old dog making itself comfortable.
Like the dog, he sometimes twitches in his sleep, whines
and mutters until his wife wraps him in her arms, rocks him back,
back, away from his dreams.

The Queen's Hospital, Sidcup

After hell, it seemed to me a sort of heaven—
the rolling wooded hills, the trees
supremely solemn and upright,
the unpocked lawns, no terror
from horizon to horizon,
in all the out-of-doors
a blessed silence.

And oh, the cleanliness of sheets!
The plenitude of milk, floating with cream,
Gillies' good humor wafting through the wards.
He saw us all full on, knew we were men.

We suffered through our surgeries
together, sometimes rejoiced together,
joined in anger at the letter from a girl
who'd tired of waiting. We fed the chickens,
milked the cows, learned together
the solitary trades—including needlework,
of which we were ashamed, despite
its beauty. Our bandaged football team
posed for its photo.

I know I'm almost handsome now—
a few distinguished scars, a Roman nose
I chose as Gillies' favorite. My mother says
I don't quite look myself, but even she agrees
the man's an artist.

I would have stayed forever.

Two One-Eyed Men

The left-eyed Duke of Montefeltro, fearful of friends
on his right at dinner, had a portion of his nose's bridge
cut out so he could watch them with his one good eye,
foil their attempts to poison him.

Private Mallard, in profile, had the same notch
when he arrived at Sidcup. A sniper's bullet
did the job on him, took the left eye too,
left a pug and somehow perky nose beneath it.

Such a lost boy he looks at first, his tender curls.
But with each surgery his face gains scars,
grows older, angrier. With his one good eye,
he watches.

Metamorphosis

Cocooned in bandages from eyes to chin,
he could only point at what he wanted—
though what he wanted from the first,
I knew, was me.

He couldn't, like some others, tease and smile,
call me the dark-eyed beauty minding the counter,
beg me to meet him after dark, behind the store,
but from his gaze, I knew.

What did he hide beneath his cottoned silence,
his sorrowing eyes, the tortured lines
of his undamaged forehead? I had a friend, a nurse;
she checked his records.

He'd had his lips sheared off along with chunks
of cheek, his nose knocked sideways,
while bringing in a stretcher case two months ago.
His midface was a mass of scars.

Eventually he spoke, though with a snuffling.
His nose was back in place, as prominent
(he said) as ever. His mouth was fixed forever
in a frown.

But when at last his eyes smiled, the blue brilliance
of a dragonfly flew from them and alighted
in my heart. For all our forty years it stayed there,
shimmering.

Private W. Ashworth

Whence comes this gentleness?

I've seen the Tonks pastels, the mass
of scarlet tissue masquerading as your mouth,
opened on the Somme.

I've seen the photographs, the slow return of light
to your pain-haunted eyes, and the last pastel where,
white-collared, you look a cleric, a good-humored saint.

Were you a happy man before? Your eyes say maybe,
but maybe your new mouth can only smile.

The Airman

for First Lieutenant Ralph Lumley, Royal Flying Corps, age 25

He'd usurped God's heaven, had shrunk God's earth, as no man should without an agonized ascent. Easily, joyfully, noisily he did it, exulting as the other's planes burst into bloom like great chrysanthemums.

And so the Holy Ghost in tongues of fire, petrol-soaked, alighted on his face. No mere nine hours on the cross for him but fifteen months of agony elsewhere before arriving at the Queen's, his face an aerial landscape of borrowed skin, rivers of blood visible beneath. His staring right eye and the absence of his left are sunk in two round craters. Something like a pig's snout lies beneath them, and below, five large white teeth protrude like pillars from the always open lake of mouth, its banks swollen.

At the Queen's, tiny gains and losses, until a chest flap is transplanted to his face at his insistence, too soon for the soft-hearted surgeon. But, *mira-bile dictu,* "by the eighth day, foul dressings having been removed, the graft has taken in a most remarkable manner."

Unhappily, the melted paraffin applied too hot, the new face blackens. He rots bit by bit, becomes the shrinking ground. They move him out of doors, into a hut.

Did he murmur *Father, forgive them* as he gave up the ghost?

"Right Eye Continually on the Roll, Seeking Moisture"
from case notes on Lieutenant Lumley

Rain down your tears, ye daughters,
on this white mask, this mass of grafted skin,
these lidless staring eyes.

Weep, weep, all ye peoples, gather your tears
for the eyes of the lidless, who can never again
not see.

The Man Who Hid from Mirrors

From a child he hated mirrors
              how they swallowed
everything they saw   jumped out
           at him in shops   showed him
a face his mother kept insisting
             was his own

                In town
he found where mirrors lived
             and kept his distance
learned to shave
        by touch alone

War exploded   and he joined up
      with his friends   The training sergeant
warned them   *Over there*
      beware of mirrors   *The bloody Boche*
have snipers everywhere

The next few years   the hell he traveled through
      required no reflection   only action
A stretcher-bearer   he gathered men
     from fields so full of corpses
          he trod on them   to lift the living

A special torment were the ruins of faces
        On leave   or in his sleep   they leapt
at him and so   he took to trembling
     his mind   blank
      until his vision vanished   altogether

Confronted   with a mirror
     he saw   nothing

Studio for Portrait Masks

Latin Quarter, Paris, 1917–1920

1.

Plaster casts of faces line the walls,
each suspended from its own crucifying nail.
It's the cast of a horror film, mouth and chin
a gaping hole, ragged scar emptied of eye,
nose a piece of shapeless slapped-on putty,
doughboy absent the smiling mouth.

Approach them with tenderness.
They were men once.

Make a miracle of masks,
send them on their way, rejoicing.

2.

An American beauty welcomes the poor beasts
into her garden, leads them through a courtyard,
ivy-laden, filled with statues she has summoned
out of marble. Searching each face
for some redeeming grace, she finds
the princes in them.

3.

It's no simple business, this healing.
No *Go and be thou whole,*
no single kiss.

Smother the living face in plaster.
Instantly make an airway; some may recall
mud's suffocation. The full horror
must be made manifest, all that's present,
all the absences.

Let the pale face dry, gentle it from its nail,
bear it before you in cupped hands,
place it on the altar in your studio.

4.

Cover it with clay and sculpt
a new one—the photo-face, in fact
the old face, with all its features now,
and all its normal imperfections—
chanting, *Come forth,*
come forth.

Slowly a face arises,
Lazarus-like.

Mold and remold it until a man
can see himself in his own image.
Then, on that life-like clay, cast
a mask of copper, thin as a lady's
visiting card, to cover only
the unspeakable.

Affix it to his face with spectacles,
painstakingly paint his skin tones,
his shaven cheeks. Hair by human hair,
create eyebrow, eyelash, moustache.
Breathe into it the breath of life

And send him from the garden.

Stay of Execution

In hospital they hid mirrors from me
but I saw the shields they raised
to block their vision, how their eyes
met only my eyes and censored out
the rest. I hid from mirrors too
until they made me my old face again,
to cover up the other.

But summer came, and sun shone hot
on tin. Unmasked, I moved deep into woods
where no one saw me, I saw no one,
and no one heard when I awakened
screaming.

Always my pistol with me.

I'd passed a meadow once, and walked there early
after such a night, thinking to die
out in the open air.

And then I saw the lark. She saw me too.

And sang.

My Wild One, Broken-Winged

Always that false half-face between us,
in day's light, and by the evening lamp.
His mouth was still the same sweet mouth,
his seeing eye as clear. He would not kiss me
with that same sweet mouth; we were polite,
like strangers.

In bed we fit together still, two spoons,
he with his back to me, his tin face hanging
from the bedpost. My body spoke, but his
did not respond, and so I learned to sleep
until, his mind crawling with horrors,
he called out, and I cradled him.

We both were starved. Some days he'd leave
before daybreak, come home after nightfall,
leaf-mould on his boots. I did my daily tasks,
walked in the woods and fields, for my own comfort
gave what aid I could to lost and fallen creatures.

One day I thought on how he'd gentled me,
his patience with my frightened virgin flutterings.
That night I stroked his tousled hair, and then,
night after night, tip-fingered further
down his face—the unmarked plain of forehead,
silk of eyebrow, eyelash, hillock of closed eyelid.

And slowly on, to crevices of scars, smooth socket
of an absent eye, the humped and unfamiliar landscape
of his nose. At last I touched his open lips—
He groaned, and rolled, and pulled me to him.
We fed each other then, wrapped in the dark.

Homecoming

You took me as your son
but he is long gone

off with his mates
eating sleeping
laughing in their deep
narrow
grave

How could you know me

There once was a lad
but he is no more

No, Will is gone
Will oh willow
Will O

You thought I would be the same
sweet Will sliding
knife into soft—

Shoot that rat before he gets our dinner!

Who's that on the stairs?
Will, is that you?

The Comforter

He's lost his face, and since his mind is gone,
they've left him with this travesty of features.
You'd think the other madmen
would nightmare at the sight of him
but no, they corner him, tell him
all the secrets they can't bring themselves
to utter, a brother's shattered head,
a German bayoneted in the back and then a twist
but no way to remove it, and on and on
the groaning.

Happily, the faceless man can't hear
beyond the noises in his head, can't see
at all. They sit close to him, or kneel at his feet,
their heads upon his lap. Sometimes he rests
an absent-minded hand on them,
as if in blessing.

Speechless

He used to love tongue, felt no revulsion,
as his city wife did, at the giant slab
lying gray and quiet at the butcher's.

He loved the taste of it, the texture,
the way his wife, out of love for him,
cooked it, her complaints comical.

They were united in their love of words,
the passionate volleys and returns
tumbling over each other.

Now, to his amazement, she's still here,
preparing foods that he can swallow
without a tongue to guide them.

They write notes, read each other's eyes.
Their bodies speak together more often
and more clearly than before.

But how they miss the rapid ease
of crossfire, the passionate exchange
of muscle in their mouths.

My Husband, Now and Then

after André Breton

My husband whose hair is fallen weeds grown over with mould
Whose thoughts are rotting flesh
Whose mouth is a window seldom opened in a fetid room
Whose teeth are skeletons dancing on reddened fields
Whose tongue is a dulled dagger
The tongue of a general in the ninth circle of Hell
Whose tongue is pulled out daily

My husband whose eyelashes were once a fluttering curtain
Whose eyebrows were arched doves
My husband whose temples were water on a windless day
With no swallows swooping
My husband whose shoulders were a steaming bowl of soup
Were potatoes, leeks, turnips, onions
My husband whose wrists were oxen
Whose fingers were angels singing in the night
That were caves of comfort and a nesting place
My husband whose calves were wild horses running
Whose feet were hymns of gratitude

My husband whose face now is a cratered landscape
Whose throat contains legions of horrors
My husband whose chest is filled with screaming horses
And echoes with their hoof prints
And his gunshots
My husband whose chest is shadowed by the moans of men
Whose belly is a drum chanting *Kill kill kill*
Is a communion cup

My husband whose nape was of antler velvet
And of a sighing note in a sonata
My husband with a back of open rolling country
With grass bending
And light like the first morning
My husband with the thighs of thunderstorms
That are dark and rolling and jealous

Filled with joyous shouts
And sudden fire
My husband whose rump was luscious fruit
Whose rump was a sonnet and a bawdy ballad

My husband now with the sex of a fallen orphan
With the sex of a line on a printed page
My husband with his sex deleted
Whose arms are of ice on a distant mountain
And a fusion of marble and schist
Whose legs are stumps
In a thousand acres of deforestation

The Broken-Faced

Like elusive birds, we're rarely seen,
despite our numbers. We blend
into deep woods, shrubbery,
pull cage doors tight behind us.

But when the light is changing,
or in early morning fog, you may catch
glimpses, enough to make you wonder
what it was you drank last night
before you staggered off to bed.

We will invade your dreams, slather
you with mud so you awake,
gasping. Another night,
you will not recall yourself.

When you boast of your country,
say war's a glory, we will breathe cold
on your neck, the words will shrivel,
your tongue blue.

When the hounds of war bay you out,
slash at you with iron claws,
we will be there waiting,
ready to take you in,
one of our ruined brothers.

Notes on the Poems

Inspired by case notes and photographs, some of these poems include factual descriptions of the surgeries. The human stories they tell, however, are largely products of my imagination.

"Transformation": This poem is based on a photograph of Private A. J. Seale, age twenty-three, wounded April 4, 1918. After seventeen surgeries (none of them performed by Gillies), he had a chin and had been fitted with dentures but was unable to chew because his lower jaw could not bear the pressure. Both his disability and his facial disfigurement were rated severe when he was finally discharged from the Queen's in November 1922, after repeated discharges and readmissions.

"Private Fairweather, Age 22": In fact, Private Walter Fairweather's surgeries occurred during two separate hospitalizations (see the introduction, p. xviii). A member of the 2nd Lincoln Regiment, he was wounded in France on the deadly first day of the Battle of the Somme, in which many "green" troops, barely trained, were utilized because casualties had already decimated the ranks. I have wondered if his apparently unquenchable sense of humor (seldom detectable among the hundreds of photographs in the archives or the sketches for them) might be attributed to his being injured in an early assault, invalided out of action, and therefore not being exposed to the prolonged battle stress that many survivors experienced. In any event, he must have been a born optimist, like my own mother.

"The Queen's Hospital, Sidcup": The facial description at the end of this poem was inspired by the final photograph of Private Sidney Beldam, age twenty. The game played by the football team was, of course, soccer. Beldam was wounded on November 28, 1917, at Passchendaele, where the quantity and depth of mud were legendary, and he lay wounded in the mud for three days before he was picked up by a stretcher-bearer who, noticing that he twitched slightly, said "This one's alive." Gillies, who performed the corrective surgeries, describes them in detail in *Plastic Surgery of the Face*. Beldam became Gillies' chauffeur, and he and his wife met at the Queen's.

"Two One-Eyed Men": Private Mallard, age twenty, from Northamptonshire, was wounded on March 21, 1917, and discharged in October 1918; his face was eventually restored. The more fortunate Federico da Montefeltro (1422–1482) lost his eye in a tournament accident in 1450. He was left with a huge scar but continued his active career as a field commander and the enlightened ruler of Urbino until his death.

"Metamorphosis": This poem is loosely based on the case history of Robert Davidson, a Dubliner who enlisted in the Royal Army Medical Corps and was wounded on April 28, 1916, at the age of twenty-six. After eleven operations, he was left with a large defect in his hard palate and many scars. He stayed on at Sidcup and met his beautiful future wife while delivering the hospital mail as part of his rehabilitation. Their wedding photo and one of Davidson in the 1950s are in the Gillies Archives.

"Private W. Ashworth": Like Fairweather, he was injured on the first day of the Battle of the Somme, July 1, 1916. The half-smile was indeed a permanent addition to his face; it is still there on a family photograph of him as an old man. Despite experiencing initial job discrimination in his work as a tailor and being jilted by his fiancée because of his scars, he had a happy life, marrying and fathering a daughter. He and his wife were adventurous but eventually settled in Blackburn, a city in northwest England, where he again became a tailor, working for himself.

The man who painted the portraits of Ashworth was Henry Tonks (1862–1937), a well-known artist whom Gillies recruited to assist him in designing faces as well as making sketches of and for surgery. Originally and briefly a surgeon before becoming an artist and art teacher, Tonks was one of the first in England to be influenced by the French impressionists. He painted a series of before and after pastels of many of the injured men, which can be viewed at the Royal College of Surgeons in London and online at the Gillies Archives website.

"The Airman": Lieutenant Lumley, on whose photograph and case notes this poem is based, received his burns on July 14, 1916, at the age of twenty-five, when his plane crashed in a training accident. After two hospitalizations elsewhere and several months at home with care brought in, he was admitted to the Queen's on November 24, 1917, and died there on March 11, 1918. Judging from his insistence on having the transplant performed when Gillies felt it was too soon, Lumley must have had a strong will to live, but he was also addicted to morphine, as were many of those who suffered extensive bodily injuries, especially burns; it was the most effective of a very small arsenal of painkillers. Lumley died of gangrene, a lack of blood flow to an injured part of the body. The stench of gangrenous tissue often pervaded the field hospitals. The photographs of Lumley's ravaged face are hard to bear, particularly in contrast to the handsome, smiling young man in uniform he once was.

"The Man Who Hid from Mirrors": The so-called "hysterical" symptoms of shell shock—blindness, deafness, inability to speak and move when there is no physical defect causing the problem—were common in those less psychologically sophisticated times. Like the effects of today's post-traumatic stress disorder, these symptoms were responses to the unnatural horrors of war. The conditions a stretcher bearer would have encountered on the battlefield and at field hospitals are most vividly described in Lyn Macdonald's collection of accounts by and interviews with medical personnel, many of them female, in *The Roses of No Man's Land* (Michael Joseph, 1980).

"Studio for Portrait Masks": Anna Coleman Ladd, who founded the Paris studio, was a Boston sculptor, the socially prominent wife of an American physician assigned to the Red Cross in Paris. She learned her mask-making technique from Frances Derwent Wood, a well-known artist who, too old for military service, volunteered as a hospital orderly before he founded the Masks for Facial Disfigurement Department at the 3rd London Hospital. Because production of the masks was labor-intensive, relatively few men received them. Ladd's masks, made of copper, were of higher quality than the tin ones produced at the 3rd London (called the "Tin Noses Shop" by the men), but were no more successful in the long run. See Caroline Alexander, "Faces of War," *Smithsonian* (February 2007): 72–80.

"Stay of Execution": Suicides must have been frequent among those whose facial wounds left them grotesquely disfigured. There was little internal or external support for these men, losing their faces before they even knew who they were, unable to find work unless they were tucked away somewhere out of sight. Many, of course, were rejected by girlfriends and fiancées. Some never contacted their wives and families, fearing their horror and possible rejection and the shock for their mothers. On the continent, where there were no institutions for facial repair comparable to the Queen's, the disfigured more often appeared in public and in the art of the time, especially that of the German Otto Dix. In France, the Union of Disfigured Men (*Union de Gueules Cassées*) was formed four years after the war by two facially injured veterans, who purchased a country estate where such men could live with their families, either temporarily or permanently. It is still in existence at Moussey-le-Vieux, with forty-seven rooms. In Germany, the pacifist Ernst Friedrich (1894–1967) published photographs of facial disfigurement in his *War Against War* (1924) and displayed many of them in the First International Anti-War Museum in Berlin until it was closed by the Nazis in 1933.

"My Husband, Now and Then": The form of this poem follows that of André Breton's "Free Union."

Photographs

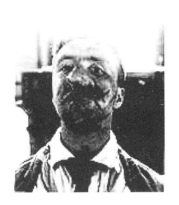
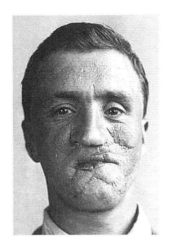

Top left: Davidson on admission, June 1916; top right: Davidson at discharge, March 1919; bottom left: Wedding photo of Davidson and his wife (the photographer retouched his chin), n.d.; bottom right: Davidson in the 1950s, at a hospital fête. Gillies faces the camera in the background.

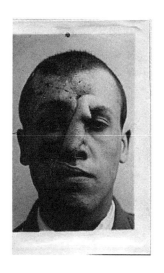

Top left: Beldam on admission for corrective surgery, June 1918; top right: Beldam with pedicle tube, July 1918.; bottom left: Beldam, final photograph, September 1920.

Top left: Beldam at his wedding, 1925; top right: Beldam and his wife, 1965; bottom: Beldam with his granddaughter Marilyn, a four-generation photo.

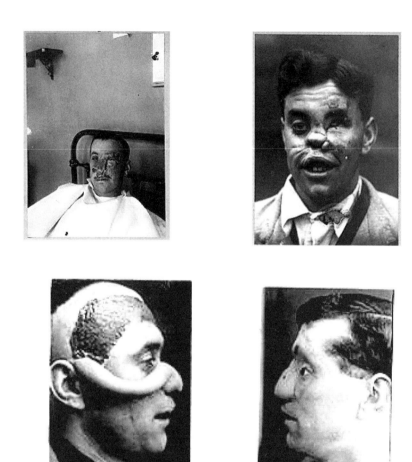

Top left: Fairweather on admission, July 1916; top right: Fairweather, January 1917; bottom left: Fairweather in February 1921, with pedicle tube, which Gilles had constructed in January; bottom right: Fairweather after final surgery, May 1921.

About the Author

 Before flowering as a poet on Whidbey Island, Washington, in the early years of the twenty-first century, Ann Gerike was a graduate student in Glasgow and London for four years (the 1950s); a faculty wife, mother, and university press book editor in Lincoln, Nebraska (the 1960s and 1970s); and a midlife graduate student, clinical psychologist (PhD, 1983), gerontologist, and anti-ageism activist in Houston and Minneapolis (1980s and 1990s). Her previous book, *Old Is Not a Four-Letter Word,* was published by Papier-Mache Press in 1997. In 2007 and 2008, she won the Stafford Prize in the Washington Poets Association contest, and her poems and stories have appeared in the *Crab Creek Review, Cascade, Soundings Review, Alehouse,* and four volumes published by the Whidbey Island Writers Association (Gull Rock Press).

Floating Bridge Press was founded in 1994. Our mission is to recognize and promote the work of Washington State poets through publications and readings. Our board of directors and editorial committee are composed of volunteers from across the community. Ask for our books at your local bookstore, or you can visit us online at *www.floatingbridgepress.org.*